WHEN YOU WERE A BABY

WHEN YOU WERE A
BABY

Text and Photos by
Deborah Shaw Lewis and Gregg Lewis

~

Design and Hand-Tinting by
Gary Gnidovic

PEACHTREE

ATLANTA

To Andrew Clarke Lewis
For always making his parents proud and for providing
the original inspiration for this book.

We would like to acknowledge all those who helped make this book possible: Dr. Maria Piers, Dr. Fran Stott, and Barbara Bowman of the Erikson Institute for their encouragement of the original idea; and our friends in the darkrooms at Photosix in Carol Stream, Illinois and Clyde Collier Photography in Rome, Georgia.

Special thanks go to all the babies, children, and family members who appear in this book and who made the photography so much fun: Whitney Barton; Blake Buford; Patrick Collier; Tyler and Laura Desper; Caroline and Rob Ennis; Jasmine Daisy Guzman; Jordan, Jeanne, and Hugh Holt; Tracy McGinnis, Jr.; Jeffrey Mathews; Candy and Mellany Murdock; Eliza and Ann Newland; Brannon, Lillian, and Terrell Shaw; Micah, Wendy, and Wade Williams; Mary Beth and Ricky Womack; Quinton and Darell Wood; Michigan and Lucy Yang; and, of course, Jonathan, Benjamin, Lisette, Matthew, and Andrew Lewis.

Published by
PEACHTREE PUBLISHERS, LTD.
494 Armour Circle, NE
Atlanta, Georgia 30324

Manufactured in Mexico

10 9 8 7 6 5 4 3 2 1

Library of Congress Cataloging-in-Publication Data

Lewis, Deborah Shaw, 1951-
    When you were a baby / text and photos by Deborah Shaw
  Lewis and Gregg Lewis; design and hand-tinting by Gary Gnidovic.
      p. cm.
      Originally published: Grand Rapids: Zondervan Pub. House,
c 1991, in series: Family share-together book.
      Summary: Text and photographs depict babies while enabling
parents to recount special memories from their child's own babyhood.
      ISBN 1-56145-102-9
      1. Infants – Juvenile literature. [1. Babies 2. Family life.]
I. Lewis, Gregg A.   II. Title.
[HQ774.L44 1995]
305.23'2–dc20

                                        94-44691
                                        CIP
                                        AC

How to Read This Book

Whenever we have family storytelling at our house, one of our five children will invariably say, "Tell me about when I was a baby."

Babies fascinate children. They wonder what they were like when they were so little. Yet when kids say, "Tell me about when I was a baby," many parents don't know what to say or where to begin.

We have written this book to help you and your child talk about the time when he or she was a baby. Not only is there copy for you to read aloud to your child, but we have also included suggestions about the kinds of things you might tell your child about his infancy. We hope our suggestions will help you personalize this book for your child.

This book is special in other ways. As you tell your children about their past, you will strengthen their sense of personal and family identity, making them feel loved and secure. And if you are expecting a baby, you can use this book to teach your children about what babies are like, preparing them for their new sibling.

Reading this book should be fun—for parents as well as children. So the next time you are tucking your son into bed, or you have a long Sunday afternoon to spend with your daughter, read WHEN YOU WERE A BABY to them. By the time you've read it a few times, we predict your children will regularly ask you to pull out this book and talk about "when I was a baby."

Deborah and Gregg Lewis

$\mathcal{E}$veryone—
    Your mother
    Your father
    Your grandmother
    Your grandfather
    Everyone you see on the street
    Everyone you know—
Everyone…even you…used to
    be a baby.

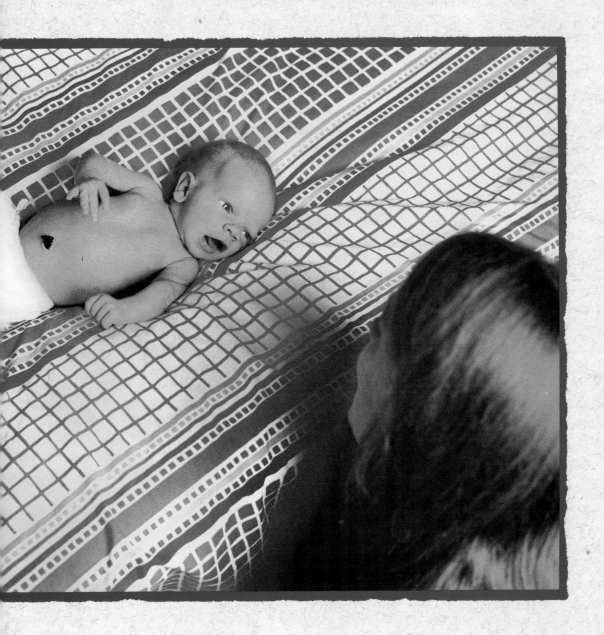

$\mathcal{B}$efore you were born, you were a tiny
baby inside your mother.

Your mother and father did not know what
you would look like.
They may not have even known whether
you were a boy or a girl.

But they did know that they loved you.

*Tell your child about your anticipation of his birth or
adoption. Describe your preparations, hopes, and
prayers. Share the different names you had picked out.*

*I*nside your mother, it was dark
and warm.
You could always hear the soft
sound of her heart beating.

But when you were born, the
lights were bright,
you could hear the loud sounds
of people talking,
and the room was colder than
your mother.

So you closed your eyes and cried.

Tell the story of your child's birth, giving details of the day, the labor, and the delivery. Include your emotional reaction to the birth and how you informed friends and relatives. If your child is adopted, share about the day of her arrival in your home.

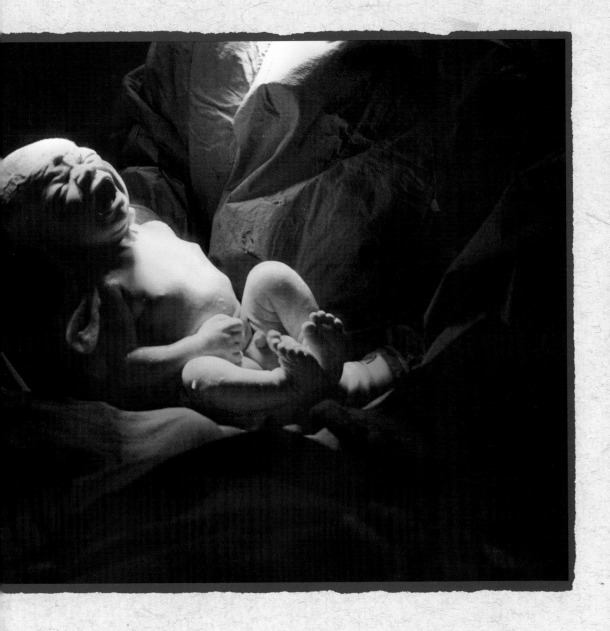

Mothers: Describe both the setting and the special feelings you experienced when you first held your child.

*A*s soon as you were born,
your mother wanted to look
at you.
She wanted to touch you and
hold you.
She counted your fingers and toes
and looked into your eyes.
She wanted to learn all about you.

And you wanted to look at
your mother.
Your favorite thing to look at was
her face.

*Y*our father also wanted to look
at you.
He wanted to hold you.
He played with you and tickled
you.
He made faces at you and tried to
make you smile.
And you liked to look at him too.

Fathers: Tell what feelings and thoughts you had when you held your newborn baby.

Tell your child how old her siblings were when she was born, and how they reacted when you brought her home.

When you were born, you were already part of a family.

Some babies have big brothers or big sisters.
And some babies grow up to be big brothers or big sisters.

*S*ome babies have
grandmothers
in their families,
or grandfathers,
or aunts and uncles
and cousins.

Your family is the
group of people
who love
and take care of you.

No other family is
exactly like yours.

Ask your child: "Who were the people
in your family when you were born?"
Tell him how his other relatives reacted
to the news of his birth.

Tell your child which of her characteristics other people commented on. Who did you see when you looked at your baby?

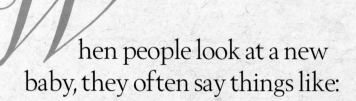

*W*hen people look at a new
baby, they often say things like:

"He has his daddy's nose."
Or "She has her mother's big
   brown eyes."
Or "He has his grandmother's
   dark hair."

When you were a baby, everyone
   in your family tried to decide
   who you looked like. And
   you probably did look a little
   like someone else.

But you looked exactly like YOU.
There has never been anyone else
   exactly like you.

Describe for your child his characteristics as an infant.

Some babies have brown eyes.
Others have blue or green eyes.
Some have fair skin. Others have
dark skin.
Some have red hair. Others have
brown or black or blond hair.
A lot of babies don't have much
hair at all.

Every baby is different
and special.
You are different
and special, too.

*D*id you know even the way
you talk is special?
No one else sounds exactly like
you.

And when you were a baby, you
had a special way of crying.
No other baby's cry sounded
exactly like yours.

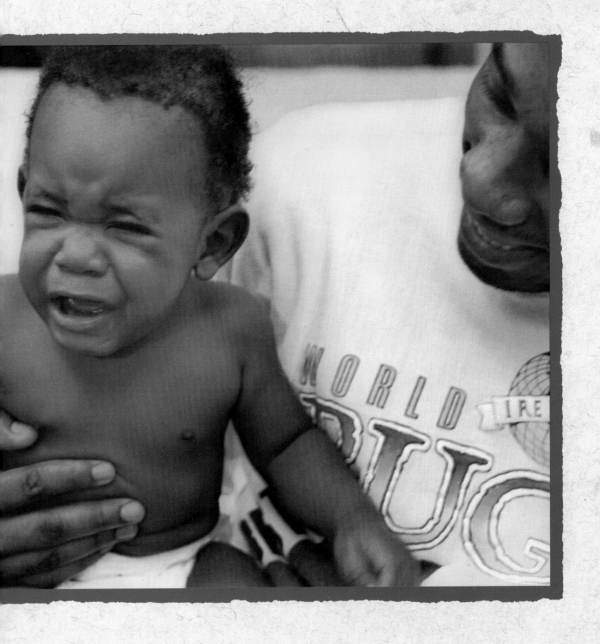

And you did cry!
Since you had not learned to talk
yet, crying was how you told
your family you needed
something.

You cried to say "I'm hungry."
Or "My diaper is wet."
Or "Please pick me up and cuddle
me."
Or "I'm tired and need a nap."

Recall for your child how and why she cried
as a baby.

*Tell about a memorable time of changing, bathing, or
dressing your baby. Or describe his reactions—either
positive or negative—to those activities.*

When you were a baby you
needed someone to change you
when you were wet.
You needed someone to give you a
bath, and someone to dress you.

Now you can do a lot of things for
yourself, but when you were a
baby you needed help to do
almost everything.
That is why you needed a family
to take care of you.

*Y*ou even needed someone to feed you.
At first you drank only milk.
Some babies drink a special milk, called
formula, from a bottle.

Tell your child how he was fed and share a memory about an early feeding time.

Other babies drink a special milk made inside their mothers' bodies.
These babies get their milk from their mothers' breasts.

As you grew, your parents
began to feed you soft foods
like applesauce, yogurt, or
mashed potatoes.
And when you grew even bigger,
you began to want to feed
yourself.

You sometimes made a real mess.
But you kept trying until you
learned how to do it.

*Tell a funny story about a mealtime, or tell your child
what her favorite baby foods were.*

When you were a tiny baby,
someone had to carry you
everywhere you went.
Then, when you grew a little
bigger, you learned to creep,
scooting along the floor on your
stomach.
Later you learned to crawl.
And then you could get where
you wanted to go even faster.

Tell your child how and when he learned to crawl or where he wanted to go.

$\mathcal{B}$ut soon you wanted to do
more.
So you began to pull yourself up
and walk by holding onto
furniture or a bigger person's
hand.

Until, one day, you let go and took
a few steps by yourself.
You fell down a lot.
But you kept trying and trying
until you finally learned to
walk.

Recall for your child her first walking experiences.

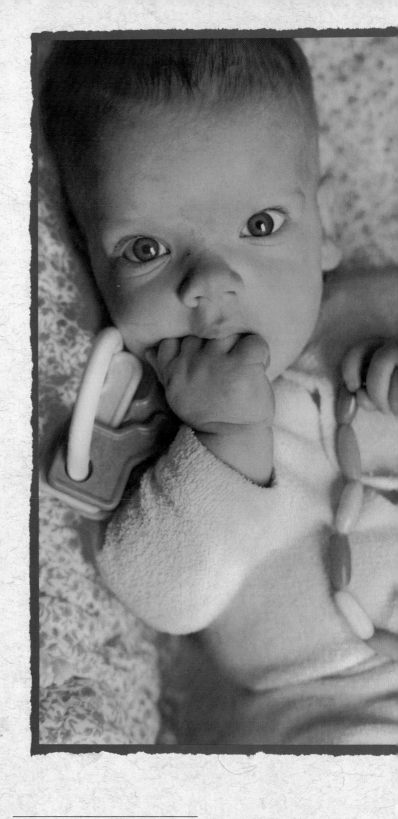

When you were a baby you
had a lot to learn.
Everything was new to
you … even your own hands
and feet.

So you played with your fingers
and toes, moving and watching
and touching them, even
putting them into your mouth.

That is how you learned that you
were you.

*Y*ou also played with your mother and father, touching their faces, pulling their hair.

They touched you and tickled you, and played peek-a-boo with you.

That is how you learned about other people.

Remind your child of special games he liked to play or songs you sang to him while playing.

When you got a little older, you
played with blocks and dolls
and trucks and other toys.
You touched them.
You put them in your mouth.
You turned them upside down
and dropped them on the floor.

Playing is how you learned about
things.

Recount for your child some of her favorite baby playthings.

Of course, playing was a lot
   of fun.
But playing is really a baby's work.
Playing is how you learned all
   about the world.

And when you were a baby, you
   did a lot of learning.
Sometimes that learning was such
   hard, tiring work that at the
   end of each day you were ready
   to…

Tell your child about a memorable bedtime, naptime,
or middle-of-the-night experience. Summarize your
nighttime routine, remind him of a favorite bedtime
story, or sing her a favorite lullaby.

…sleep like a baby.

You needed to sleep more often
than you do now.
So you took a lot of naps.
Everyone tiptoed so they
wouldn't disturb you.

Sometimes you woke up in the
night and cried.
Your mother or father would feed
you, rock you, and tuck you
back into your bed.

*N*o other baby slept or learned
or grew exactly like you.
Because there has never been
another baby just like you.
Which is why you're just as
special now as you were...

when you were a baby.